Praise for *A Love Greater Than Death*:

I remember the day I met Dori; I was amazed by how normal she seemed. To meet her you would never know that she has suffered unspeakable tragedy. Unspeakable because when the story of that day and what followed is told all the air seems to evacuate from the room. She tells her story of what God has done for her and her family with grace.

She extends that grace to all those that she encounters. She does not believe your loss has to be as horrific as hers. She is a rare believer in that she truly believes all of God's promises with a revelation that has traveled from her head to her heart and back. She believes that God's grace is sufficient for your broken heart and what He did for her He will do for you. It doesn't matter how a heart gets broken; Jesus heals the broken hearted.

As you read this story her gratitude will be unmistakable. She is truly thankful that God has healed her broken heart and set her free. By the time you have finished reading this story you too will be grateful for God's healing power.

It is impossible for me to tell you all that there is to tell about her, but as her best friend, I can tell you that everything that you will read is true. She is uniquely and remarkably normal but peculiar enough to show forth His praises for all He has done for her and will do for you.

Sincerely,
Angel Hagmaier
Attorney at Law

A LOVE GREATER THAN

A LOVE GREATER THAN

A TRUE STORY

DORI POWLEDGE PHILLIPS

Tate Publishing & *Enterprises*

and bruised of soul could understand that their life is not over just because they've been through the miry clay and horrible pit experience of Psalms 40:1-3. As she begins to reveal to you how she got a new song in her heart and how God began to establish and reinvent her future, you will be so happy you read this book of wisdom, grace, sorrow, and rejoicing. You will absolutely say, "There is a real God of grace and comfort."

While reading page after page of minor and major miracles you won't want to put this book of hope and overcoming expectation down until you have read it and re-read it at least once. When you learn how God can take you from the worst day in your life to the brightest hope you could ever imagine, you will begin helping thousands of others to get free from all bondage of depression, trauma, fear and defeat that are at epidemic proportions in our society and world today.

I am not sure what I can add to Dori's story of magnificent grace and recovery, except to say that in all my thirty years of pastoring churches, I have never seen a more remarkable miracle of God than the one you have chosen to read, study, analyze, then share with someone else. You should prepare yourself now to be so motivated and inspired that you'll constantly begin to think and say, "Nothing will ever be impossible for me to do from this day forth!"

I promise you that having observed and read this brilliant work of real life recovery, you will forever believe that your best days are ahead.

It is very important to me which books I write a foreword to or endorse. Dori's book is so powerful that it makes you feel endorsed by a loving God when you read it. As I observed Dori's story, I got it! My life was highly impacted for success in all circumstances and knowledge of how to live life like a child of God at all times and through any experience.

Dori, do not thank me for penning this letter for your book. I am so humbled that you would allow me to. Let me thank you for asking me to put my name in this most precious book of triumph in tears. I am forever grateful to you for your daily determination to let God be glorified in every aspect of your life.

For the thousands who are about to be changed by this book – I am sincerely,

Walter Hallam, M.Div., Theology
Senior Pastor, Abundant Life Christian Center
President, ALMOND Ministries
La Marque, TX

Introduction

I stood in the crowded room with family gathered around and conversations taking place all at once. In the midst of all that was happening, my cousin, Jackie, whom I have always liked because of her quick smile and infectious laughter, began to share her story with me. She told me that she had accepted Jesus as her Savior eight months prior at the Celebration of Life for my family. She had originally only planned to attend the short graveside service in the morning and not go on to the church for the memorial service, had I not said something that compelled her.

At a complete loss for what she was talking about, I asked her what it was that I said to her. She reminded me of how she had approached me that morning and said, "Dori, I am so sorry."

My response to her was, "It's okay. We are going to laugh a little and cry a little, but everything is going to be all right, because I have been wrapped in the arms of Jesus."

Come with me on this journey of loss and tragedy, faith and hope, and see the supernatural healing power of my God. He has made what is a common tragedy to man an uncommon miracle in my life. So sit back, get comfortable, and prepare yourself to laugh a little, cry a little, and experience being *wrapped in the arms of Jesus...*

October 18, 2005

As I was getting ready for work, moving around my house as quietly as possible because Adam and the kids were still sleeping, I couldn't help but laugh at how everyone had been rearranged from the night before. We liked to call it "musical beds." On a regular basis, the kids would all start out tucked in their beds and by morning Isaac and Rachel would be in our bed. Adam would then resign himself to the fact that he was only going to get sleep if he moved to the couch. Jake and Blake, now ten and twelve, would stay in their own beds or sometimes "sleepwalk" to the couch. At 6:30 a.m., I was off to work as usual. The hour may have been early, but truthfully it was really so late. If only I had known just how late the hour was for this chapter in my life, maybe I would have changed everything. The hours and minutes of this life tick by, giving no thought to those who wished they could push pause before an appointed time. But time goes on, life goes on.

Adam called me at work around 8:00 a.m. It was his scheduled day off and he was home getting the kids ready for school and, of course, could not find Isaac's uniform pants to save his life. I wasn't able to help him much from downtown Houston, but you know how that goes: mom is expected to have all the answers, no matter the logistics of things. Isaac was finally ready and as they were pulling out of the driveway, Adam called to say he was sorry for getting frustrated about Isaac's lack of clean school pants, discussed his plans for the day to clean the carpet, and said he would call me when he had gotten the kids to school. "I love you," he said. "I love you too," I said. Little did I know, that would be the last conversation we would have, and the last time I would see any of them, until we meet again in eternity.

My Story

Once upon a time, there was a little girl with dreams of a fairytale life. She daydreamed about the perfect little white house on a hill with a white picket fence, a wonderful husband and two children (of course a boy and a girl). Dreams of being in love and treated like a princess consumed her thoughts when she wasn't playing with her Barbie dolls or hide-and-seek with her brother.

That little girl was me: Doris Ann Miller, born June 17, 1969, to John and Cynthia Miller in a small suburb of Houston, Texas. My life took turns that certainly did not appear to be fairytale-like; however, don't lose heart, as you will soon discover how I ended up with a life of love, beauty, and joy unspeakable.

My birth just happened to fall on Father's Day, and my dad always told me I was the best Father's Day gift he had ever gotten. Dori became my nickname because that was the only way my brother, Harry, who was four years old when I was born, could pronounce it. Although my childhood was not a bad one, I recall it being lonely at times because I was painfully shy.

We didn't attend church regularly, so I would get very excited when I got an invitation to go with a friend. Church seemed to have such a nice atmosphere, and I liked being there because everyone was always so kind to me. When I was eight years old, I went to a Vacation Bible School with one of my mom's friends, Martha Knox, and I absolutely loved it. I enjoyed making crafts and playing with the other kids, and since the classes were relatively small, I never felt overwhelmed. One day, during Vacation Bible School, the pastor was speaking to us about Jesus and how he died on the cross for our sins. I didn't know who Jesus was or why he had to die, but I knew he was real. I could feel it in my heart. With my heart pounding all the way, I walked forward to accept Jesus as my Savior.

At the end of the week, I was going to be baptized. It was one of the most memorable events of my childhood. My entire family and many of the church members attended and we had a dinner afterward, all on account of my baptism. It felt so special to me, and it seemed important to everyone involved. Regardless of the fact that we did not attend church very often, my parents loved me, and I received a very moral upbringing.

As I entered my teenage years, I found that life became this huge inner struggle between doing what I had been taught and following the crowd. The entire focus for my friends and me was boys and, of course, with that came an incredible amount of peer pressure. I truly did not know the ways of God; however, I did know right from wrong, and recall desiring to be a virgin when I got married. That soon left my thoughts in high school because having sex and not being married seemed to be perfectly acceptable to everyone I knew. In my mind, I equated it with being loved. In my freshman year, I met and began dating the boy I would later marry and have three children with. I, like many teenage girls today, was looking for love in the wrong place.

Early in my senior year, I found out I was pregnant. When I was about eight weeks along, I stopped going to school because I could not deal with the humiliation of being pregnant at seventeen years old, and on top of that, not married. Even though having sex before marriage seemed acceptable in society, having a child out of wedlock apparently was not. And I felt it. When I was only about four weeks pregnant, one of my school counselors called me out of class to meet with her in the office. She told me she knew I was pregnant, and I needed to have an abortion or I was going to ruin my life completely. I had no idea how she knew because I had not told anyone. She kept calling me at home and making appointments for me at Planned Parenthood. She even told me she would go with me and that my parents never had to know. As young and scared as I was, I was afraid to tell her I did not want to have an abortion because I was certain my parents would not approve. However, my parents didn't know about the pregnancy yet, so there was no way I could go to them about this counselor's behavior. Instead, I did what any scared teenager would do—I quit school to avoid any more pressure from her. During this time, Charlie and I were not together very often, and I was lonely and scared. Maybe he was scared too. All I know is that it was not an easy time for any of my family.

I gave birth to my oldest daughter, Patricia Jean Melton, six weeks before my eighteenth birthday. Charlie and I got married by the Justice of the Peace when P.J. was six weeks old and, for a brief moment, it seemed we were on the right track. The minute P.J. was born, she became priority number one, and as much as I hated to leave her with a sitter, I went to work right away because I needed to support her. My new marriage was anything but ideal and it felt as if my life had been turned completely upside down. At eighteen years old, I had a newborn baby, a horrible marriage, and a full-time job. I was completely exhausted and in shock about the way my life was turning out—a far cry from my childhood expectations.

Regardless of my high school counselor's opinion, P.J. was one of the best things that ever happened to me, and I knew I needed to do whatever it would take to care for her. A short fifteen months later, I gave birth to baby number two—Samantha Jo—and she was precious. My marriage was still in shambles, but P.J. and Samantha were my saving grace. I loved them so much, but at the age of nineteen, I was so young and naïve and still primarily concerned about what I was going to do with me and the miserable state I was in.

After three years, I could take it no longer. The constant fighting and misery had become too much to deal with. I filed for a divorce. The girls were three and two years old at that time, and I was twenty-one. One year later, Charlie and I decided to try to make our marriage work again, and within a few short months, I knew it was a horrible mistake. Things were worse than before. However, I soon discovered I was pregnant—again. (In case you are wondering, I did believe in birth control; it just never seemed to work very well for me.) I was so sick during the early part of my pregnancy and very worried because I could barely afford to take care of the two children I had, much less another one. I decided my only option was an abortion. Other than the brief experience I had with my high school counselor, I had never really given abortion much thought one way or the other; however, during this stage of my life, I was of a mind that everyone should be able to make their own choice. When it came down to it though, I was tormenting myself with the thought of aborting this child. It just didn't seem right to me.

Until I was faced with the decision about how to deal with this pregnancy, I really had not given God much thought in a very long time. I began to have thoughts about how serious abortion really is and what my eternal consequences could be. You see, I didn't know much about God, but I did believe in Jesus, Heaven, and Hell because the only Bible verse I knew was the one I learned as a little girl during Vacation Bible School, John 3:16: "*For God so loved the world that he gave his only begotten son, that whosoever believeth on him would not perish but have everlasting life.*" I started thinking about abortion and what it actually involved—the death of a child—and how I didn't want to go to Hell for any reason. Could this send me to Hell? I didn't have any friends who knew the Lord, so I called my best friend and told her what I was thinking. She said, "What does God have to do with this?" I realized I wasn't going to get an answer to that question from her. I had only told one other person I was pregnant, and he kept telling me to get an abortion or my life was only going to get worse. Everything seemed so hopeless.

I decided to go to the abortion clinic because I felt I had no other option. I could not afford another child without a husband. Charlie took me to the clinic and even he didn't seem to feel very good about it. Once I got registered at the clinic, there was a series of steps I had to go through before the actual procedure. With each step, I went to a different room and spoke with a different person. Each time I entered a new room, it seemed as if each new person was trying to talk me out of having the abortion. I thought, *What is wrong with you people? Isn't this why I'm here?* However, I said nothing and just kept moving from room to room. The last step was to take this cup of pills that sedate you before the procedure. I took the pills and immediately went outside and vomited. I just couldn't do it. I went back in, told them I could not go through with the abortion, got a refund (minus fifty dollars for the drugs) and left. They told me not to worry because the drugs would not hurt the baby, and they actually seemed happy for me. I felt so relieved; however, that was very short lived. Once I got home, I realized my circumstances had not changed. My future still seemed hopeless. I was a single mom with two children, one on the way, not enough money to take care of them, and horribly sick from the pregnancy. I knew my only option was to go back to the abortion clinic. Or so I thought…

That night in bed, I began to talk to God. I wasn't sure if he was interested in the details of my life, but I was desperate to know if he would forgive me or if having an abortion would send me to Hell. I thought this because I knew a fetus was a real child, since I had already given birth twice, and it seemed like murder to me. Surely murder deserves Hell, right? I was about to learn that God's view is so different from ours. I told the Lord I had no choice but to go back to the clinic, but I really needed an answer. "Will you forgive me for doing this?" I told him to flash lighting on the house or throw a brick through my window, whatever it is that he does, but please, just let me know.

I awoke during the night because God had given me a vision in a dream: it was a picture of Jesus on the cross and, like a flash of lightning, I knew the truth. God was going to forgive me because he sent his Son to die for that very reason. I didn't know anything else about Jesus, but I did know he died so I could be forgiven. At the same time, it felt as if the weight of the world had been lifted from my shoulders. I was convinced that if he would go to the extreme of death for me, then he would help me take care of this baby.

The next day, I called my parents and asked them if the girls and I could come live with them for a little while. They never asked why, but instead just said to give them a few days to get the house ready. By the end of the week, my Dad and brother came to my house with a moving van, helped me get packed, and the girls and I were off to live in the home I grew up in.

I spent the next nine months with my parents. After being there for a few weeks, I told my mom I was pregnant and explained what was taking place with Charlie and me. I wanted to know why she didn't question me when I asked to come back home. She said, "I figured if you felt the need to move back, then you must have had a very good reason and would tell me when you were ready." I have the most amazing parents. I went through that pregnancy, labor, and delivery without a husband—a natural one anyway. There were so many people who felt sorry for me, but I felt so safe living with my parents and with my newfound relationship with the Lord. I did not feel sorry for myself. It taught me a valuable lesson about how things on the surface are not always what they seem.

After Jacob was born, I went right back to the old way of life—the party scene. I didn't know I was supposed to read the Bible in order to get closer to Jesus, and I was terrified to go to church. (I'm not sure why, except I was very intimidated by the thought of going. It's funny how much

I loved it as a child and how my perception had changed since becoming an adult.) I had just had an incredible encounter with the Creator of the universe and had no idea what to do with it.

By the time Jacob was a year old, I was the most miserable person on the planet. I was twenty-four years old, and Satan and this world had managed to rob me of every good thing I had ever believed in. I no longer believed that there were good men in the world, and I certainly did not believe marriages could really be happy. My little girl dreams of being a princess and having a prince charming had been completely destroyed. I began to cry out to God in my heart for help. I was desperate—and then I met Adam…

Our Life Together

As I pulled up in front of my neighbor's house to pick up P.J. and Samantha, I couldn't help but notice the very good-looking guy playing basketball with his two young children. My friend came out to the car and said, "He's a cutie, huh?" Of course I agreed and she told me he was single. I was way too embarrassed to get out of the car and meet him, but I agreed that she could give him my number. I had been a single mom for three years and was pretty burned out on the party scene, so I wasn't dating anyone. The girls were now six and five, and Jacob had just turned one. After many separations and reconciliations, I finally had to admit that my marriage to the kids' father was just not going to work. I was a broken-hearted, twenty-four-year-old with three small children and had resigned myself to the fact I was either going to stay single or settle for mediocrity, because at this point in my life, I no longer believed in happy endings.

Well, having said all that, three days later, I received a call from the hunky guy in the neighborhood, whose name, by the way, was Adam. We talked briefly, and he asked if he could call me again. After he called me several times over a period of a week, I finally decided I would ask him to stop by because it was obvious to me he wasn't going to mention it. He said yes and was at my house in about thirty minutes. I had to laugh at myself because at nine o'clock at night, I was putting on more makeup and trying to look cute when I normally would have been taking the makeup off and wearing comfy clothes for bed.

I will never forget the moment when I answered the door and saw Adam up close for the first time. He was even more handsome in person, and we both smiled at each other. Neither of us was disappointed. I knew at that very moment this was the guy for me. I couldn't explain it; there was just a connection between us that was instantaneous.

We began dating right away. Adam was a twenty-seven-year-old single dad with two children: Amber, four, and Austin, three. Between the two of us, we had five children all under the age of six—instant Brady Bunch—almost. Because we were single parents, we already had so much in common. The kids were very important to us both, and we started trying almost immediately to figure out how to blend a family. Adam was only separated from his wife, and at first I was really concerned about seeing a man who was still officially married. I didn't want to get in the way of a marriage, and I also didn't want to get my heart broken. He assured me that things were over between them, and that his wife was already with someone else, so the divorce was just a formality. Needless to say, with five children and two ex-spouses, we had a lot of baggage in our lives that would unfold little by little throughout our life together. However, at this point, we were just so happy to be with each other.

After several weeks of dating, Adam began to tell me how he had turned his life over to Jesus about one year prior. He had been raised in the church and to know the Lord but had never really committed in his heart. He had gotten heavily involved in the party scene which sent him down a spiraling path of chaos. As you can imagine, this didn't do anything good for his marriage or help him as a parent. Life had really changed for Adam since his commitment to serve Jesus with all of his heart and he taught me so much about the Word of God. We started going to church and teaching our children the ways of God. It took a little time, but we made changes in our life and were able to create a lifestyle that worked for us and gave us confidence that we were leading our children in the right path.

Through the next couple of years, Adam and I had a baby together (a whopping ten pound, four ounce baby boy, Blake), got married (in that order I hate to admit—issues of life we were still working out), and blended a family of six children. The beginning was very tough because we seemed to always be facing financial difficulties, dealing a lot with the other parents, and trying to grow in our walk with God as well as growing up all at the same time. However, no matter how difficult things were, Adam and I had a love for each other, a love for our children, and a love for the Lord that enabled us to keep moving forward.

Within four years of Blake being born, we had two more children, Rachel and Isaac, giving us the sum total of eight kids! Most people thought we were crazy in a nice sort of way, but our kids were so close and we had learned to make things work in such a way that life really had a pretty nice flow to it. While having the babies, I had been able to stay at home with them for five years and I was so grateful for this time, because I loved nothing more than being a wife and a mother.

In 2001, we moved to League City, Texas, where all of Adam's family lived, and started settling in. By this time, I was working full-time again for a law firm as a legal secretary, and Adam was working as a pipefitter for a chemical plant. The kids were in school, except for our two youngest ones, and I had managed to work part-time for a little while to get to be with them before they were off and running with the others.

Life began to get a little hectic due to the fact we had kids in high school, junior high, and elementary with activities ranging from cheerleading, volleyball, Boy Scouts, and Little League. Needless to say, we were spread pretty thin. Adam was such an amazing father, and he was always with us one hundred percent of the time. He did his part as a parent, so it made life much easier on me. We really began praying and seeking God about the fact that everyone was so scattered and life was beginning to feel like it was only about running from one event to the next. Adam and I made a decision in 2004 to put our kids (all of them—except for Amber and Austin because they lived with their mom) in the private school at our church. We really did not have the money for that but felt in our hearts that it was right and just started trusting the Lord to make a way. We contacted the school and they gave us a nice discount and worked out a payment plan. Just like that, the kids were starting school at Abundant Life Christian School in the fall of 2004.

The three oldest, P.J., Samantha, and Jake, were furious with us about this decision. I can understand why it may have seemed irrational to some, but as parents, you have to see beyond the here and now and do what is best for your children in the long run, which will sometimes not necessarily line up with how they see it. I am grateful to be able to report all of the kids were so happy after the first few weeks and agreed it was the best year of their lives so far.

Life seemed to be really flowing smoothly as we began the school year in 2005. However, only a few weeks after school started, a category five hurricane (Rita) was headed straight for the Gulf Coast. We lived in Galveston County and were placed under a mandatory evacuation. We loaded up, took two cars, the four youngest kids and our Lab, Holly, and headed out toward New Braunfels, Texas. In our little caravan were also Adam's sister, Laura, and her family, and his brother, Steven, and his family. Needless to say, with six adults, nine kids, three dogs, and a cat, we were a pretty hilarious sight. P.J. and Samantha decided to go stay in the dorm at the University of Texas in Austin with one of their friends, and Amber and Austin were staying in Houston at their home with their mom and step-father, since they lived farther from the coast.

The trip started out to be somewhat of a nightmare due to the fact a panic hit Houston and 4.5 million people decided to all leave town at once. It took us nineteen hours to reach New Braunfels, a four-hour destination on a normal trip! We arrived exhausted but safe. We had to stay gone for several days, so it turned into a mini vacation, and we had a wonderful time. The hurricane ended up making a turn and we only had a bad storm with very minimal damage to our area. We returned home and life resumed its normal routine. Or so I thought that was how it was going to be.

The Fateful Day

Approximately one month after returning home, on October 18, 2005, I received the worst possible news that you could ever be told—*worse than any nightmare I had ever experienced or imagined.* I had gone on to work that morning and was awaiting Adam's phone call after dropping the kids off at school. That call never came. I began to get a little concerned after not hearing from him for several hours because it was just out of character for him not to keep in touch when we had a plan. I decided to call the school and check on the kids. I spoke with the secretary and told her, "I know this is going to sound funny, but are the kids at school today?"

She said, "No, Dori. Only Sam." I knew then that something was horribly wrong, but I still did not think it was what I was about to hear. She asked me to hold on and transferred my call to the school principal. The principal picked up the phone and said, "Dori, there has been an accident. We just received a call from the Texas City Police." I asked her what happened. She said, "Well I don't know how many people were in the car." I could tell she knew something and did not want to say it. I told her that *I knew* how many people were in the car and insisted that she tell me what happened. She said, "*Dori, there were five fatalities.*"

I could not believe what I had just heard. I was completely stunned and in total disbelief. All I could say was "not my babies." I put the phone down and had no idea what to do. I had never felt more helpless in my life. I walked into my bosses' office and told him what I had just been told. He couldn't believe it either. In a matter of minutes, the entire office was at my desk and everyone was scrambling around trying to take this in. It all felt so surreal, as if I had stepped out of my life and was watching this happen to someone else. One of the partners took charge of the situation and removed me from the crowd to wait in his office. He said, "Just sit tight. We are making some calls and are going to get to the bottom of this."

All I could do was say the name of Jesus. I began to ask Him these questions: "Jesus can this really be happening?

We love you and live for you. Surely this could not happen to us? Jesus, where are you?"

In a matter of fifteen minutes, David walked back in and said, "We are going to meet the Texas City Police at your church with your pastor." I knew then that the truth had been confirmed. My sister-in-law, Andrea, who also worked downtown, came to my office and rode with me to the church. Her presence in the truck was such a comfort. I began calling close family members to tell them what had happened and that they needed to meet me immediately at the church. Everyone I called was either falling apart or trying to say that it could not be true. There was no good or easy way to handle this situation. I just needed them to get there.

On the drive to the church, the only person I wanted to speak to was Jesus. I knew he was the only one who had the answers in this situation, because he holds the key to life. I had spent the last twelve years getting to know Jesus through the study of the Word, prayer, and other life circumstances, and I knew I could trust Him implicitly. All of a sudden, I began to see a tornado in my peripheral vision. God was showing me that the whys and why me's were all swirling around in that vortex and, if I chose to go down that path, I could get caught in there and possibly never make it back out. So I made a decision. "Okay Lord. I understand what you are saying. I'm not going to question you or ask you why or why me, but you have to help me because I can't do this." The truth of the matter is that I didn't really want a good answer. A good answer would not have been good enough. I wanted this whole thing to go away and not be true.

There is never a good answer for why a tragedy happens—that is what makes it so tragic. If we choose that path, the whys and why me's will only lead to anger and bitterness and ultimately end up destroying our lives and more than likely, the lives of those around us. I really had no idea what the Lord was about to do for me and how powerful my God really was. But I was soon to find out.

I arrived at the church at approximately 3:00 p.m. The accident had happened at 8:55 a.m. and it took all day to clear the highway and to find out who was actually in the car. So, by the time I drove past the location of the accident, I could not tell where they had been or what might have happened. For that, I am so grateful. My pastor was standing outside waiting on me when I arrived. He put his arms around me, and I began to cry. It felt like a protective daddy holding me. His strength held me up, and he ushered me inside where the police were waiting, as well as some family members and members of my church. My pastor told me what happened first and then I was questioned by the police. I think, in the back of my mind, I had some small hope that this could be changed, but when they started asking me for dental records in order to identify my family, I knew that they were truly gone. It was as if my future had been snuffed out in a moment of time. I could hardly see past the nose on my face and had no idea even how to imagine what the next moments would hold, much less tomorrow.

I had one question burning in my mind, and I was desperate to know the answer. I believed the reason I was born on this earth was to be a wife and a mother and had never really aspired to be anything else, and to have it all taken from me so quickly left me questioning myself. I asked my pastor, "Could I have done something wrong?"

He spoke very intently to me and said, "No. Don't you ever think that. You didn't do anything wrong, and this is not about you." I wanted to drop my head and tell him he was wrong because this felt like it was all about me. My entire life had vanished in the blink of an eye. But I looked at him with trust and received his words of truth. When I did, the lies that were coming at me were completely shut down. The truth is, we live in a fallen world and bad things happen to good people every day. And secondly, this was not about me. It was about Jesus Christ and the power of the cross, what he will do for you and through you if you will let him. If our focus is only on ourselves in a situation, it causes the truth of what has really taken place to seem very foggy.

It is so important to have a pastor (Hebrews 13:17), a leader in your life with God's wisdom, who can speak truth to you when your circumstances have you feeling so muddled that you can't see it for yourself. I believe it saved my life that day. If I had believed the lies that I had done something to deserve this, I know I could have lost my natural mind that very hour. This circumstance was way too big for me to handle alone. I needed God and his truth and wisdom to rescue me. And that was exactly what I received in the very first hours through the voice of my pastor. My God was fighting for me, and I did not even know it—yet. The Bible says in Psalm 20:1–2, "In your day of distress may the Lord answer you, may the name of the God of Jacob protect you, *may your help come from the sanctuary...*" (Emphasis mine.)

As I was leaving my church, the truth of what happened had really begun to sink in. There was not one part of me that did not hurt, even to the point of feeling physically achy. In the accident, the car malfunctioned causing the throttle to stick and the brakes failed to overcome the speed. Adam tried to get the car off the road, but the speed and lack of control of the vehicle were too much—they ran into a pole in the median causing the car to split in two and explode on impact. There was no one to see, nowhere to go, and absolutely nothing I could do. It felt as if my husband and babies had just vanished into thin air.

As I was walking outside to the car, I remember the atmosphere had a pink, hazy look to it. Even the trees looked odd and out of shape. I was trying to get my vision focused on the ride to my mother-in-law's house, not understanding what was happening to me. I went to sit outside in her backyard because the weather was beautiful, and it felt less claustrophobic out there. After a very short time, I began to feel a tangible presence of God which started from my feet and slowly moved its way up to the top of my head. I had never experienced the grace of God quite like this before—it was as if I were in a protective bubble and it made me feel very safe. Once his presence reached the top of my head, the atmosphere immediately cleared. I knew then I had just been *wrapped in the arms of Jesus.*

Pain can distort our vision and cause us not to see our circumstances clearly, the way we were meant to see them. However, if we will allow the comfort of the Lord to touch our pain, we will begin to move forward in a healthy pattern. Otherwise, we may wake up one day, years down the road, wondering how we ended up in a place so far away from what our lives were meant to be. We see life through the eyes of our experiences, yet when we allow God's Word to take precedence, we can view it from the perspective of eternity. His ways and thoughts are so much higher than ours.

That night, after the crowd had dissipated, and I had no choice but to lay down, still stunned and numb from the events of the day, I did the very thing I told the Lord I would not do. My mind began to scream "Why, why, why?" over and over again. Almost as fast as it started, the Lord spoke to me in a very loud voice: "Be still and know that I am God" (Psalm 46:10). Immediately, every thought and question left my mind. I believe when you make a decision to cry out to God for help, the Creator of the universe can command your thoughts to go. I felt protected by the Lord—He is our very present help in time of need (Psalm 46:1). However, I would not be telling the truth if I said I slept like a baby. My sleep was achy and fitful, but my mind stopped the pattern of thought it had begun to go down, enabling me to rest.

The Revelation

The next morning when I woke, the house was already starting to fill up with people—friends, family, church family—all there to take care of our needs and be a comfort to us. I decided I needed to get in the shower and forced myself to get the day started. As I was showering, I couldn't understand how I was even functioning. I felt so incredibly horrible, but yet I was still able to take a shower, communicate with others, and even think rationally. Life hurt so badly that I asked the Lord to please allow me to still have the ability to see beauty and to have compassion for others. I didn't want to be blinded to everything around me by this overwhelming pain. Still standing in the shower, I finally asked the Lord, "What is wrong with me? I feel so bad, yet I know it should be incredibly worse. How come I can even stand in the shower? Why am I not lying on the floor just wanting to die?" The Lord answered me immediately and said "*O death where is your sting? O grave where is your victory?*" (1 Corinthians 15:55). (Emphasis added.) I could hardly believe what I had just heard. As a believer in Christ, I knew what the cross represented and had believed for twelve years that Jesus died a sinless death so we could be free and have eternal life. However, that morning the Lord made it so real to me and had given me something solid to hang on to.

I got out of the shower, got dressed, and even put on my makeup. It's amazing what we will still do in the midst of a tragedy. With my hair wet and holding a towel, I stood in the living room amongst all of our visitors and made a declaration, "Jesus did what he said he did on the cross, and he is who he says he is. *The grave will not get the glory for my family!*" I may have looked like a crazy woman with my hair wet and holding a towel, but I had never been more sure of anything in my life. There is a power that raised Jesus from the dead and it was alive on the inside of me. That same resurrection power was holding me up when my circumstances said I should want to lay down and die. I knew then that everything I had believed in was true. Because of the work of the cross, my family was *alive.* They were not going to come back to me here, but I knew ultimately I would have them for all of eternity.

With this declaration came the decision to make changes to the "traditional" funeral. With the understanding that my family was alive, I refused to spend any time at all in the funeral home—no viewing. I was not going to sit around all day and stare at five caskets. That just felt very unhealthy to me. I also made the decision to have the graveside service first and then the memorial service at the church in the early afternoon. I had a horrible vision of a long procession of cars travelling down the highway to the graveyard. That signified something I did not even believe. It is amazing what we do out of routine or just because it is the "acceptable" way. Since I knew my family was alive, I was not going to glorify death but instead, celebrate their lives. I planned to end our day at the house of God.

This new plan gave us all something to do, and quite frankly, I think it was a welcome distraction. Everyone involved began looking for special pictures to make a video, deciding on songs, and contemplating how this "Celebration of Life" should go. I was so grateful for all of the family and friends who were working so hard to make this come together. I tried to go through pictures, but I really did not have the ability to accomplish even the smallest of tasks. My mind and emotions felt so shaky. For the first time in my life, I had no appetite as well. I could hardly even bring myself to drink anything. Life felt so surreal.

I spent the rest of the day being close with family and friends, crying, laughing, praying, and talking. Once again, it was time to try to sleep. Going to bed was so difficult because I missed them so badly, and our lives had just been shaken to the core. Samantha was sleeping with me, so that was somewhat of a comfort for both of us. My body felt so achy, almost as if I were coming down with the flu. However, this was no flu. I was in for the fight of my life—the fight of faith.

Changing My Mind

As I awoke the next morning (day two after the accident), the pain was still there—full force. The mornings were so hard because I would wake up and realize this had not just been some terrible nightmare but in actuality, the nightmare existed while I was awake. I spent so much of my time thinking, since this was all I had to do with Adam and the kids gone. I was trying to figure out what in the world I was going to do with myself now and what kind of life I could possibly have without them. As I lay there, I thought about what I heard people whispering the day before, "She's in shock, she's in shock." All of a sudden, a panic almost hit me that I could possibly be in shock. I asked the Lord, "Am I in shock?"

He immediately answered back, "No. I'm with you." I was so relieved, because I could not imagine leaving the horrible place I was in and sinking even lower. Remember I had been given the earth-shattering revelation just the day before that my family was alive in Heaven. However, this was uncharted territory for me, and Jesus was building my faith as I walked out each day.

Jesus felt so close, I sometimes expected to look up and find him sitting next to me. I didn't have to pray in the way we normally think of praying. I simply spoke to him, and he answered. He was so present in my time of need. I finally understood what it meant when Jesus told Paul, "My grace is sufficient for you, for my power is made perfect in weakness" (1 Corinthians 12:9). No matter how large or small the situation, the grace of God is able to cover it perfectly. When we are very weak, as I was, his power is made perfect.

So relieved to not be in shock, I continued to lie in bed quietly as most of the house was still sleeping or perhaps pondering their own thoughts as I was. My next line of thought was how a woman had once told me what it was like for her when she lost a very close loved one. I had only lost elderly grandparents and a relative who was a little more distant, and it had not affected my daily life. This woman said that she actually had a physical pain in her chest. I slowly moved my chest back and forth checking to see if this pain had arrived yet. I know it sounds funny, but surely this would have to happen when your husband and four babies have just died, right? I felt the grace of God with me, but surely today I was going to want to die. Isn't that what was supposed to happen? What the Lord spoke to me next absolutely changed everything for me. He said, "Do not expect to receive what anybody else has experienced. Let me walk you through this." I immediately understood what he was telling me—stop expecting everything bad you have ever heard happen to others and just follow my lead. He changed my thought process, which is vital to any progress we will ever make in this life.

I told him, "Okay, Lord, I hear what you are saying. I agree to walk with you and see what happens." As far as I could tell, none of the rest of us seemed to know what to do. I knew I was not the first person to experience a tragic loss like this, but I had never personally heard of a situation like mine that had a good ending. So, walking with Jesus was definitely the most appealing option.

Over a period of twelve years, I had grown so close to the Lord and had walked out many situations with him. I knew how much I was loved by God, so I felt very secure with this decision. However, I had no idea what his plan was or how my life was going to turn out. Romans 12:2 says, "*Be not conformed to the ways of this world but be trans-*

formed by the renewing of your mind so that you may know what is the good, the acceptable and the perfect will of God." (Emphasis added.) Transformation takes place in our minds first and then we can see our circumstances clearly. The greatest day in our lives is when we will allow the Lord to change our minds. This is how our circumstances are affected—not by God changing the situation. He changes us first and then we walk according to his plan and purpose to live a healthy and prosperous life, regardless of what situations and circumstances come our way.

From a Tragedy to a Miracle

Four days after the accident, and we were still making plans for the Celebration of Life and spending time with family. I don't think I was actually accomplishing anything. Even the smallest of tasks was mentally and emotionally exhausting. I found myself sitting alone for a moment with my thoughts, which had become routine over the past few days, and the Lord spoke to me, "I can turn this tragedy into a miracle just like that." It was as if I could hear him snap his fingers. I answered back, "Yes, you can." I didn't know how he would do it, but one thing I did know was that my God was able. As it turns out, I would not have a long wait to discover what the

Lord was talking about. The miraculous was just around the corner…

Day seven arrives. A day I had been anticipating and dreading all at the same time—the burial services and the Celebration of Life for my family. While lying in bed that morning, I began talking to the Lord. I felt so afraid. Jesus was so gentle with me and my emotions, and I could feel him close. I said, "You haven't left me yet. Please don't start today." At this point, I was still uncertain about how long this grace was going to last.

The burial service was to be held at 10:00 a.m., and the drive was about forty-five minutes long. The kids and I rode in one vehicle along with my mother-in-law, Mary, and brother-in-law, Jason. When we arrived, there were already so many people there—approximately five hundred. I specifically requested that only family members and close friends attend this ceremony. I had wanted the majority of the people to attend at the Celebration of Life service.

As we pulled into the location where Adam, Jake, Blake, Rachel, and Isaac's bodies would be buried, I felt so afraid of how I would feel when I saw the caskets. However, God always knows what we need to combat any situation. Standing at the end of the walkway was my grandmother, Nanny, waiting for me. She is the sweetest woman, with a strength that goes deep. She locked arms with me, and we headed down the walkway until we reached the tent. As I looked at those five caskets, all various sizes to fit my husband and babies, I realized that everything my family had believed for the last twelve years was true. The power of the cross had overcome death. There was no longer a sting that could destroy me. Adam, Jake, Blake, Rachel, and Isaac were all alive and well in Heaven. Those five caskets, with such an ominous presence, did not have the ability to destroy me or hold me down. I was so relieved and incredibly amazed at the truth of the Word of God.

My pastor spoke for a few moments and delivered the Word of God to all of us. His love and compassion meant so much to my family and friends. Over the past seven days, the love of family, friends, and even those we did not know very well served to bring comfort and healing to us, and we were all so grateful. Even though the grave did not have control over me, I still did not like it, nor did I want to spend much time there. We left within one hour of arriving.

The service at the church was to begin at 2:00 p.m., so we had a small amount of down time. As I sat in a chair at my mother-in-law's house, I could not hold back the tears. I missed them so much and life felt achy and painful without them. I knew in my heart I would get to spend eternity with my family, however, there was going to be a process to go through in order for my broken heart to be mended.

We arrived at the church to find that fifteen hundred people came to support and show respect to our family. My church seats approximately thirty-five hundred, to give you an idea of the size of the sanctuary. There were people from all walks of our life—family, church members, Boy Scouts, Little League, school, and work. Flower arrangements lined the walls of the sanctuary and all across the front of the stage. The foyers were full of flowers and it had even gotten to the point that the church staff had to put flower arrangements in their offices. The flowers signified life and made the service so beautiful. In front of the stage, there were exhibit boards and tables for Adam and each of the kids. The boards were decorated with pictures of their lives, and the tables were covered with items they each held dear. This allowed everyone to get a glimpse of how precious Adam, Jake, Blake, Rachel, and Isaac actually were.

We started the service with several worship songs. It seemed so odd to me and my children that we were all sitting down during worship (we always stand in our church services). It was at that moment I realized this was not a church service and we had invited people here to be a part of our daily life. So the kids and I decided to do what we would normally do and stand together and worship the

Lord. We stood and lifted our hands to Heaven as we sang, "When I Think About the Lord" and simultaneously all fifteen hundred people stood up in unison. It was an amazing sight to behold—this sea of people honoring the Lord for my family.

My brother-in-law, Mike, delivered the eulogy and he did a wonderful job depicting our family life. Then Steven and Jason, my other two brothers-in-law, spoke together for a few moments and shared their thoughts. Then, our four oldest children, P.J., Samantha, Amber, and Austin all stood together and expressed their gratitude to all of our family and friends. What was so amazing to me was that we had all lost the ability to wear a mask. So often, we mask who we really are and project to others what we think they are expecting. Not so this day. Everything that might have bothered me the week before was no longer even a concern. Maybe that should be an eye opener for all of us. As we walk through our daily lives, we can get so caught up in the stresses and cares of the day we live in that we can lose sight of what is truly important, like sitting with our spouse and enjoying a quiet conversation, reading a book with our child, or coffee with a close friend. We should make a conscious effort to focus on the positive and not the negative aspects of our lives. Otherwise, we will speed through life having never actually lived but only existed.

A beautiful video was shown. I then spoke for a few moments and expressed that the only reason I was able to stand was because my Lord was holding me up, and to acknowledge my gratitude for the incredible love and support that had been extended to my family. I told the congregation that although you can never be prepared for something like this, we were prepared for eternity. I learned through this time if you will prepare for eternity, then you can deal with anything that comes your way in this life.

My pastor spoke last and shared the Gospel of Jesus Christ. He addressed the people with wisdom to begin to bring understanding and healing for this type of situation. He made an altar call and approximately two hundred and fifty people accepted Jesus as their Lord and Savior! The Lord turned my tragedy into a miracle—just like that. I never cease to be amazed by my God. A day that should have been the worst day of my life ended in complete victory. Only God can take a situation that is so horrible and devastating and bring beauty and victory to the surface.

Being Still

I awoke the next morning, seven days after the loss of my husband and babies, having no clue as to what I was going to do with my life. The services were over, and it was time for everyone else to go back to their routines. I knew I shouldn't make any hasty decisions, because I could feel the frailty in myself. I was shaken to the core over the loss of my family and life as I knew it was no more. I was still at my mother-in-law's house and could not even fathom the thought of going back to my home. I was just not ready to face their things. I had taken a leave of absence from work until the end of the year. I asked the Lord, "What should I do?" He answered me very clearly, "Be still before me and exercise." I understood what he meant by "be still" but I was a little taken back by the exercise part. Surely he wasn't worried about the extra twenty pounds I'd gained over the last six years right now? I then realized as a practical matter, exercise does so much for us mentally. The Lord wanted my mental health to be strong, and exercise was a vital part of keeping it that way.

To be still before God means to spend time in his presence. I had so many people calling me and saying things like "Dori, you can't let your mind be idle. You've got to get back to work right away." Or "Maybe you should go to Bible college. You've always wanted to do that." It is in our own wisdom that we think the mind always has to be busy. The Lord was trying to clear my mind and bring me to a state of complete calm.

The way to enter into the presence of the Lord is through worship. I would sit on the couch with a worship music CD playing softly and very quietly just tell the Lord over and over, "All I need is you." I really didn't have too many other words to say. There was so much pain everywhere, and that was the best I could come up with. I thank God every day our words are not always what he needs, just our willing heart. As I would sit with him in worship, I could feel the word of God come to life like never before. In Isaiah 61:3 it says that "He will give us beauty for our ashes, the oil of joy to replace mourning and a garment of praise to replace the spirit of heaviness." It was as if I could feel healing oil being poured over my body and little by little, day-by-day, the pain began to subside.

I now understand why we sometimes try to suppress pain. There are types of pain that are so overwhelming they have the ability to win in our lives and take over. However, I found that when we cry our tears and release that pain in the presence of God, he will not allow it to overcome us. The Bible says in 2 Corinthians 4:8–9 that "We are hard-pressed on every side, yet not crushed, we are perplexed, but not in despair; persecuted, but not forsaken; struck down but not destroyed." Although circumstances may occur which cause us to feel hard-pressed, perplexed, persecuted and struck down, it is very clear that God's plan for our lives is to overcome. In his presence, these things are all possible.

He Never Changes

It was nearing the end of the second week without Adam and the kids, and, quite frankly, I was just trying to get through the days and figure out what I was supposed to do about life. I was still staying at my mother-in-law's house and spending a large amount of time with my thoughts. As I was pondering my life, the Lord interrupted my thoughts and spoke to me, "Your life has been radically altered, but I have not changed. I still came to give you life and life abundant." I was not expecting this and could hardly believe what I was hearing. I immediately answered and told him I believed his word, but he would just have to show me how I was supposed to live an abundant life. I had no idea how to do anything anymore.

Without my husband and babies, every step I took was new and still very painful.

The Bible says in Malachi 3:6, "I am the Lord. I do not change so that you O descendants of Jacob are not destroyed." I began to understand he was telling me that even though my world had been completely rocked, his plans and desires for my life had not changed. In John 10:10 Jesus says, "I came that you would have life and life abundant." I knew that these things were true, but I was having a hard time seeing it because life was so painful, and I missed them terribly. However, I made a decision to believe the Word, and I had the hope that just like in times past, Jesus would come through for me in this circumstance as well.

The beginning of achieving abundant life is the understanding we deserve to have it. Once I was able to grasp the truth of that, even under tragic circumstances, I began to look at my future differently. Even though at the time I did not feel very happy or up in my mood, I was able to look ahead and hope for a future full of joy unspeakable. It is so important in difficult situations to stand on the Word of God. The Word is alive and active and very present in our time of need. It will combat your negative situation and you will begin to feel differently on the inside.

The Path to Freedom

I was now entering week number three, and life was still so hard. However, Jesus was with me and holding me every step of the way. As each day passed, and I gained new revelation and understanding through the Word of God, I could feel myself getting stronger in my will and able to keep moving forward. We were starting a conference at my church that week called Camp Meeting on the Coast. It is a conference held each year which starts on Sunday and lasts until Wednesday, with two services a day. It is a huge event, and we have guest speakers come in from all over the country, as well as ministers and other churches arriving from all over the world. Little did I know just how impacting this event was going to be for me personally.

I arrived on Sunday morning with our four other children, P.J., Samantha, Amber, and Austin, as well as many other family members. We were all sticking very close and comforting one another, trying to make sense out of what had just taken place in our life. I still felt very achy and fragile, however, when I was at my church, I felt safe and protected. I know the kids all felt the same way. I found it difficult to laugh or make jokes, which normally came very easy for me. It seemed as if there was a weight on my shoulders I had never experienced before. Through all of this, I felt an inner strength which I knew came from God, from knowing him over the past twelve years. I had been feeling like I needed to go back home—almost like I was drawn there. However, I was so afraid to face my house and all of their things.

By the end of the service that morning, the Lord spoke very clearly to me to go home, and everything was going to be all right. I knew I needed to trust him. So, Samantha and I headed back home. P.J. lived with her dad at this time, and she went back there but was coming over almost every day. Amber and Austin went back to their house with their mom because they needed to get back to school. Amber was a junior and Austin was a freshman at Hargrave High School in Huffman, Texas.

Once back at home, Samantha was able to get situated in her bedroom and bring some sort of familiarity back into her life. I just closed the doors to the kids' bedrooms, and would only use my bedroom to change clothes and shower. At night, I slept on the couch. For the time being, we had found a level of comfort we could live with. My brother-in-law, Jason, stayed with us for about a week to try and help us acclimate back into our home, which was now very different. We also had Holly, our Labrador Retriever, who was about a year old.

On Monday morning of the conference, after spending my first night in my home since the accident, I was sitting in the coffee shop at our church and talking with my friend, Lee. I heard many different people referring to the deaths of my family as being premature. I never really questioned that or gave too much thought to it. However, I heard it spoken on quite a number of occasions since the accident. The Lord began speaking to me as I sat there waiting to walk into the sanctuary. He said "*Premature death? Premature death?* If your family died premature, then you did something wrong, and I addressed that on the first day. You don't understand eternity. Not you or the rest of the Body of Christ—and I understand that—but you have to know that I never left you." I started telling Lee what the Lord was saying to me.

She asked me, "Do you think it was the plan of God for Adam to die at thirty-nine years of age?" I didn't believe it was the plan of God for my husband and children to die in an accident, but I knew God was trying to reveal something to me—something very important.

In my study of the Word of God, I found that the Bible references premature death for the Christian only in instances when he refuses to get out of sin and his life ends before it should have because of his own actions (1 Corinthians 5:5). For the sake of simplicity, one example could be when a person refuses to quit smoking and then he gets lung cancer and dies. That would be considered premature death because this person may have never experienced this if he would have quit smoking. In this instance, smoking is the sin because it is harmful to the body, which the Bible describes as the temple of the Holy Spirit (1 Corinthians 6:19).

I walked into the church thinking about what the Lord had just spoken to me. I found a place to sit, and praise and worship began. Right after praise and worship, the person giving the announcements told us to walk around and give people hugs and be friendly. I call this our "meet and greet." I started to say hello to a lady, but she turned around before I got a chance to. I then saw this woman headed toward me, and she stopped when I looked at her. She seemed very hesitant and cautious. I stuck out my hand and said "Hi. I don't believe we've met before." She pulled me close and gave me a hug. As she did, she whispered in my ear, "I pray for you every day. Your witness strengthens me. I too have treasures in Heaven." It seemed like an odd sort of thing to say to a stranger, and normally I'm not comforted by someone I don't know, but this woman seemed different for some reason. I knew something special had taken place in those short moments, but I was unsure as to what it was.

I took my seat, and my pastor was about to begin his sermon for the offering. He always does a short teaching before taking up the offering because he wants people to understand why they should give according to the Word of God. Pastor said, "Turn to the book of Job." Before he said what passage to go to, I flipped it open to Job 38. And as I looked down and began to read, the Lord was speaking through his Word to me. Job 38:1, "Who is this who darkens counsel by words without knowledge?" (For me specifically, the Lord was referring to the comments about premature death.) "Now prepare yourself like a man and I will question you and you will answer." Verse four: "Where were you when I laid the foundations of the earth, tell me if you have understanding." And then verse twelve, "Have you commanded the mornings since your days began and caused the dawn to know its place?" I answered and said "No, Lord. I haven't." Simultaneously with turning to this passage of Scripture, the woman who had hugged me earlier tapped me on the shoulder and handed me a bookmark entitled "The Weaver." It reads like this:

> "My life is but a weaving between my Lord and me. I cannot choose the colors he worketh steadily. Sometimes he weaveth sorrow and I in foolish pride forget he sees the upper and I the underside. Not til the loom is silent and the shudders cease to fly will God unroll the canvas and explain the reason why the dark threads are as needful in the Master's skillful hand as the threads of gold and silver in the pattern he has planned."

Okay, Lord, I understand what you are saying. Even though I do not understand everything that has taken place, you never left me. When the Creator of the universe makes it very real that he never left you, then it really doesn't matter what the circumstances are—even if you lost your entire family—it doesn't get any better than that. You cannot go up from there. The highest place you can be in this life is with God in control. So I told him, "I understand what you are saying to me, and I believe you never left us. But, you told me in the very beginning of this that the accident was a violent attack against the Kingdom of God, not against me personally, but against your Kingdom (Matthew 11:12). Well if that is the case, then that means Satan got to my family. If you were in control, then how was Satan able to attack my family?" It would not be long until I would get my answer...

The following morning, Tuesday, as I was waking, the Lord began speaking to me, "Just like my Son, Satan was pushing and driving to kill the Messiah. But I was in control and I had a plan. The day of the accident, there was spiritual warfare taking place, but I was in control, and I still have a plan."

I was stunned by his response. God clearly uses his Son Jesus as our supreme example and what he did was remind me that just because things don't work out the way we think they should does not mean he has lost control of our lives. When we place our lives in God's control, he not only knows how to maintain it but also sees a much bigger picture than we do. Remember, we still live in a fallen world. When we accept Jesus Christ, then we personally have been redeemed from the curse in the earth, but this world is still in a state of havoc and it has not yet been made new. The Bible says one day we will have a new earth (Revelation 21:1), but for now we have to learn to live in this fallen environment.

Set Free

It was the final day of Camp Meeting on the Coast, and I was sitting in the sanctuary of the morning service taking in all that the Lord had spoken to me. At the end of the service, I felt a release come from the center of my chest and a physical weight lift off of my shoulders. I immediately said, "Lord, what did you do?"

He answered back, "Who the Son sets free is free indeed." (John 8:36) I had been set free from the burden of the loss of my family in twenty-three days! I was amazed at the love and power of my God. God is not bound by time, and he will bring us along as quickly as we will allow him to. I understood what the cross represented, freedom from all that has us bound, but I never even thought to ask for freedom in this circumstance. I mean, seriously, how do you get free from that? And, more importantly, do you want to be free from losing your husband and babies? Sometimes we choose to be bound because we don't feel we deserve to be free, as if our suffering somehow causes our difficult situation to hold its value—this is nothing more than the guilt Satan tries to put on us.

I knew that since the accident my mind was not thinking as clearly as usual, but I also understood that I was in a life and death situation—either I was going to live or lie down and die with my family. I hung on to Jesus with all I had because I had nothing else to hang on to. This served to work to my advantage. If we cling tightly to Jesus, he automatically does what is in his nature to do—set us free from all that has us bound. He set me free from the horrible burden of my loss by the truth that Adam, Jacob, Blake, Rachel, and Isaac were truly alive, and one day, I would get to be with them forever.

I began to study out these scriptures to gain more understanding of what the Lord had done for me. John 8:32 states, "You shall know the truth and the truth shall make you free." Then in verse 36 it says, "If the Son sets you free you shall be free indeed." I didn't understand what the scriptures were saying, "Did the truth set you free or the Son?" Then the Lord took me to John 14:6 where Jesus states, "I am the way and the truth and the life..." Then it all fell into place for me. If you will know

Jesus then he will make you free because he is the truth, and when the Son sets you free, no one will ever be able to take it away from you.

The key to being free is having a personal relationship with Jesus Christ. Very simply stated, the way to do that is to read the Bible—a little bit every day—and then you will learn and find out the true nature and character of God. You will begin to understand that you can speak to him, and he will speak to you. Just like in other relationships, there is communication, and it takes time to develop.

I was now free, but this did not mean that my heart was no longer broken. Being set free meant I was no longer bound by the huge burden of the loss—nothing short of a miracle for sure. The healing process would prove to take a little longer—over a period of the next eight months. That evening, I felt like I could laugh again. I actually made a joke to one of my friends about Adam being really busy in Heaven taking care of all of the kids. She looked at me and said, "Well, it looks like I'm starting to see some of the old Dori come back." She did not know what had happened yet, because truthfully, I was still receiving and understanding what was taking place myself. All I knew was I was so grateful for the love and power of the cross of Jesus Christ enabling me to feel a hope and a future.

His Burden is Light

About a week later, I was sitting in a Wednesday night service the day before Thanksgiving, when my pastor began to talk about paying a price for ministry. He said, "I don't care who you are, if you are called to preach the gospel, then I guarantee you that you will have paid a price for that gospel." This statement really impacted me and I started thinking about paying a price. The next day, I was at home just talking with the Lord and I told him, "Setting aside the preaching of the gospel, this was a very heavy price to pay in this life—for anyone. What I want to know is how come it doesn't feel as heavy as I know it should?"

The Lord answered me, "I told you, my yoke is easy and my burden is light." (Matthew 11:30) Once again, I was astounded at the Lord's response and the simplicity of the truth of his Word. Only God has the ability to make you feel just the opposite of what your circumstances are.

In Matthew 11:28–29, Jesus is speaking and says, "All you who are weary and heavy laden, come to me and I will give you rest. Let me teach you my ways because I am gentle and humble in heart and I will give you rest for your souls." When you come to the Lord and allow him to teach you his ways, you will find that he is so gentle. Through my entire walk with God, and especially through this time, he was incredibly gentle and understanding with my every emotion. God will never try to break you. He will only love you and build you up. His desire is to give us rest for our souls, which are our mind, will and emotions. This allows us to rest easy in a world which is continually bringing stress, pain and all sorts of emotional upheavals.

I can personally attest to the fact that these scriptures are real and true, because if they were not, I would not be writing this book. I would be locked up somewhere completely lost and out of touch. Without the supernatural grace and power of God, a human being does not have the ability or strength to combat a situation like this that is so much larger than life.

Healing and Forward Movement

When I received the news that Adam and the kids had not survived the accident, I didn't think I would ever be able to breathe without immense pain or feel normal again. The pain was so excruciating, I had no idea how I was going to ever function in this life again, how I would be able to think, speak, eat, or live normally. However, when I cried out to Jesus, he took me to the secret place. A place deeper than I had ever gone, and wrapped his arms around me while I cried rivers of tears. As the days would go by, and the tears began to subside, the pain was also subsiding. I found that when you cry your tears in the arms of Jesus, and when he removes pain from your life, it is real and it doesn't have the ability to come back to you. The healing you receive from Jesus is permanent because of the power that is still present from his sacrifice on the cross. I did not deny the pain or pretend it did not exist. I simply rested in his presence until he lifted it off of me.

This healing was truly amazing and almost unbelievable if I had not experienced it myself. Once healed, the Lord begins to restore everything that was lost along with your tragedy until he makes you whole again. Jesus turned my broken road into smooth pavement with beautiful scenery along the way. It is our choice whether we will accept what he has to offer and receive it. The only thing to get in our way from receiving the beauty of the cross is our own belief system which says we cannot have something so good and true.

In God's timing, you will receive understanding in bits and pieces along the road of recovery. If we will open our hearts to Jesus, every day will hold new revelation and deeper understanding of ourselves and in turn allow us to help others in their journey. In this journey of self-discovery, it is imperative that we lay those things down that hinder our healthy progress. It may mean walking away from relationships that are damaging to our souls. Sometimes the best decisions are the most difficult. *Lord, help us to make right choices and hear your voice clearly.* It is so important in the healing process that you do not allow yourself to take on the beliefs of those who do not line up with the Word of God. Separate yourselves from those who are trying to put the world's belief system on you and who speak contrary to the Word. I struggled with this because I did not want to hurt anyone; however, I came to understand that there were some people in my life who did not want to see healing and progress come to me because of their own pain and disappointments. I could not fix them and knew I had to walk away in order to keep moving forward. You cannot stay in a stagnant place in order to please others. That will never help anyone. Keep moving forward and pray for others always.

Pushing Me Forward

Once I made the decision to return to my home, about three weeks after the accident, it was time to face the music. My husband of twelve years, Adam, thirty-nine, and my precious children, Jacob, twelve, Blake, ten, Rachel, seven, and Isaac, six, had passed into eternity, and they were not coming back here. The Lord set me free from the burden of the loss by the truth that they were alive, and corrected my belief system about his plans for me and my remaining children, so now it was time for the healing process to begin.

Initially, I liked thinking of Adam and the kids in terms of a group. It was much easier to see them as being together and sort of pretend that Adam had just taken them somewhere. No way did I want to break them down individually and let the pain in my heart emerge to the surface any more than it already was. It is amazing what the mind will come up with to protect itself. However, the Lord had other plans on how I was going to get through this.

My first instinct was to run as fast and as far as I could. China would've been nice, but fortunately for me, I did not have the funds to escape to China. The holidays were immediately upon us, and I couldn't bear the thought of being here without them for Thanksgiving, Rachel's birthday, Christmas, and New Year's. So, in my desperate wisdom, I planned a trip for me and the kids and a friend of mine and her kids to all travel to Colorado and go skiing for Christmas. Doesn't that sound lovely? Well, as one could expect, our plans began to fall apart at the seams. Okay Lord, I see you're not going to let me run. "Trust me," is all He would say. I was so afraid to face the holidays. I didn't want to buy any gifts, put up a tree, or decorate at all. I just didn't feel as if I had the energy or the strength of heart for it. Christmas was my family's favorite holiday.

I was beginning to settle into a routine; however, I only used part of the house—the kitchen, living room, the master bathroom, and my closet. I didn't feel like I could face all of the kids' things in their bedrooms. Samantha was using her bedroom and bathroom.

Then one day, about three weeks before Christmas, all of the kids were home and we were getting ready to go somewhere with my brother-in-law Jason—or at least that is what he told us. I had just gotten out of the shower and was getting ready when the girls told me there were Christmas carolers at the door. What? In the middle of the day? I went to the door and it was a precious lady named Georgeann who worked for Jim MacInvale at Gallery Furniture. All of our friends and family sent letters to Gallery on our behalf for their annual furniture giveaway, and we were chosen. All of a sudden, furniture was being moved out of my house and into the garage and new furniture was brought in. There were reporters from the *Galveston Daily News* and *Houston Chronicle* and so many people from different walks of our life. Samantha said it felt funny because she knew all of the people, but they didn't belong together. In their unconditional love for us, they came together to bless our family in a very special way.

Once all of the furniture was in place and everyone had left, it was time to go through the kids' personal belongings, since their furniture was no longer in the rooms. My very dear friend was in town and she stayed to help me, which made it so much easier. Through many tears that day, I continued to receive healing from the Lord and make progress.

I realized that God has his ways of pushing us forward when we get stuck. And I had definitely gotten stuck. This very special gift allowed me to move forward and begin living in my home again. I had a brand new bedroom suit, so my bedroom now had a totally different feel. I was able to sleep in there again. They gave me a new couch and coffee table, as well as a dinette set. Also, each of the kids got a new bed and dresser. I thank God for givers. Our giving is so important in the process of life.

Rachel

Christmas was around the bend; however, Rachel's birthday was even closer. With December 16 looming ahead, it brought my baby girl to the forefront of my thoughts—she would have been eight years old. The week leading up to Rachel's birthday was very difficult. I loved having a "little" girl in the house. Our other three girls were all in their late teens and busy with their lives. Rachel would go shopping with me, and she was always involved with anything I had to do around the house. I was so excited about having her. I knew for years to come I would have my baby girl to do all kinds of fun things with, and I could really focus on her since she was the only girl in our younger crew of kids. She and I had already discussed plans for her birthday. She even asked me if we could have her birthday party this year without the Christmas tree! I told her I would do my best. Rachel informed me one day while we were at the mall that she was the only one of her friends who did not have a Build-a-Bear. So, we decided to have a party there; however, that was not going to happen after all. It was so heartbreaking to me because it felt like she was missing something. This, of course, was my human understanding and pain talking. *Miss something here while living in Heaven? Who was I kidding?* Talk about knowing how to throw a party and, of course, Jesus spares no expense. She could have all the Build-a-Bears she wanted.

About two days before her birthday, I arrived home to find a very cheery bouquet of flowers sitting on my doorstep. A mom-friend had left them there with a note saying these were for Rachel's birthday and that my little angel had not been forgotten. It was gestures like these that would first bring tears and then healing. Unconditional love heals the heart with tears that set you free. By the time her birthday arrived, we all decided to go to the crosses where the accident had taken place—there were five crosses, one with each of their names on it that we had received as a very special and most treasured gift. We brought balloons and talked and prayed and then released the balloons to Heaven. This was my way of taking a step of faith and releasing my baby girl into the hands of the Lord. I knew he would take good of her until I would meet her again in eternity. This was how the Lord led me to face the temporary, yet very painful loss, of my baby girl.

Christmas

Now it was time to address the issue of Christmas. I decided to handle it a little differently. Life was very different, and it was okay to treat it as such. I bought gift cards for all of my nieces and nephews instead of doing any real shopping, and I stuck with all of our routine holiday plans. I would sit with the Lord at home and cry because I missed them so much. Then I would get up, dry my tears, and go to each event that we normally attended: my grandmother's house with all of my extended family the Saturday before Christmas, Adam's mom's house with his brothers, sisters, and my nieces and nephews on Christmas Eve, and then with my parents and brother and his family for Christmas day. I found with each event we attended, the love we all shared for each other brought peace and healing. The Lord was showing me that with his strength, I was going to be able to get through this and continue to move forward.

Fortunately, in 2005, Christmas fell on a Sunday. My pastor decided that year to have a luncheon after the morning service for all of the people who did not have family events to go to. It was such a relief to be able to wake up Christmas morning and just get ready for church instead of having to sit around and focus on the fact that our home was silent, without the usual ruckus of anticipating Christmas, wrapping presents, and then watching them tear it all apart. P.J., Samantha, and I were able to go to church early and spend time in the presence of the Lord with people who cared for us. We felt the sense of family instead of the feeling of loss.

Afterward, we went to my brother's house, along with my parents. Amber and Austin met us there as well. I still planned a trip as my Christmas gift to the kids; however, this was not a run-for-your-life trip as the one I previously imagined. Rather, one to show them that life was still meant to be good. That evening, the kids and I went back to the house, and the next morning we were off to San Antonio for a few days.

Our First "New" Vacation

We all woke up the morning after Christmas with the anticipation of taking a short road trip. Jason was going with us as well. He was always such a blast to have around, and I think my mother-in-law may have insisted he go because she did not want us to travel alone. However, Jason was a trooper and said he would love to go.

Off we went in a borrowed Tahoe so we wouldn't have to take two cars, and we were on our way to San Antonio. A ride that would normally only take three hours took us about five. We played music, told stories, laughed, stopped several times for road trip favorites (in our family you can't have a road trip without Dr. Pepper, beef jerky, hot fries, and Sour Patch), and just in general had a great ride. We checked into our hotel and went to the River Walk in search of food and entertainment.

I packed the trip with events. We saw the IMAX of the Alamo and then visited the Alamo. We took the boat ride down the River Walk, shopped at the mall, and went to all five museums in downtown San Antonio. There was a festival going on in the streets while we were there, so that added to our fun. It was also time for the Alamo Bowl game, so the place was packed with people. We loved it. We were all very tired at the end of the trip, and I can honestly say we all felt the absence of Adam and the kids. However, we were able to see that life was still meant to be enjoyed and lived. That was the goal. Mission accomplished.

Information about Separation

During this season, I was speaking to the Lord about something that weighed very heavy on my heart. I believed in Heaven and eternity, so that was a non-issue with me. I also knew that Adam and the kids were happy and secure and I was so grateful for that. But what about me? I was going to miss out on my life with them, all of the daily moments and events that make our family lives beautiful and fulfilling. The Lord began to talk with me. He said, "You know that Heaven doesn't operate in time right?" Yes, I believe I understood that as much as I could. "So for them, they don't realize that they have not just seen you and that is why they don't hurt from the loss."

Amazing… I never thought about it like that. In 1 Corinthians 13:12 it says that "you will know fully and be fully known" (This scripture is referencing the chasm between earth and Heaven.) "This means that when you see them again, you will know them and be known by them just as you were the day you were separated. You miss nothing. Life did not end for them, and it did not end for you. You will have all of eternity to live together." The Lord continued to lift my heavy burdens. It is okay to live to the fullest without the people we love the most because in Christ, life does not end here. He was continuing to free and heal my soul with his presence and his counsel.

Jacob

With the New Year would also come Jacob's birthday on January 25. The Lord was using the holidays and my children's birthdays to address the loss of each one of them individually, but I didn't realize it yet. The week of the holiday would be very difficult, but once it arrived, I would have a feeling of freedom, peace, and joy. Jakie was so special to me—to all of us. He had a great sense of humor and was very witty for a twelve-year-old. He was also the only one in the house with amazing discipline. We used to laugh and wonder who he had gotten it from. Jake loved Jesus and was not ashamed to preach the gospel. It was his way of life. He was a talented skateboarder and was in the process of being sponsored by a skate shop. Jake spent hours every day perfecting his skating skills. His grades were straight A's, and he was very much a people person. Everyone loved him.

During this time, I received a visit from Jake's best friend's mom and her friend. They began to tell me how they understood what the Lord was doing with me because of what Jacob had taught them. Jake had been great friends with C.J. (we called him Rooster) since they had met in Little League two years prior. C.J.'s mom loved Jake like her own son, and he loved her as well. She was a great cook, so that was one of his favorite things to do at her house—eat. She told me that while he was at their house about one week before the accident, he was sitting on the kitchen counter talking with her while she cooked. He said to them, "Ms. Lynette, Ms. Laura—I have been telling you about Jesus for two years. Well, now its time." He led them to Jesus right there in the kitchen. I knew that because of this, their lives would forever be changed. Their eternal future had been secured. This was so special for me and I was reminded how much my son had impacted other people's lives. Jacob was not forgotten.

Through this healing process, the Lord was continuing to comfort me with the hope of Heaven and eternity—assuring me that this loss would only be temporary.

Isaac

The beginning of February would mean Isaac's birthday was immediately upon us. He was born on the second—Groundhog Day. My heart ached with longing for my youngest baby boy. He was the baby, and he knew it. Isaac was our little spitfire. Adam once said he figured after having seven children, we should have this parenting thing down. Then Isaac was born. He was such a unique child—sweet, stubborn, mischievous, sensitive, sneaky, funny, and he could climb like a monkey! He was also a total momma's boy. I know you should never do this, but he would climb into bed with me almost every night, and I had gotten very used to snuggling up with Isaac in the middle of the night.

During this time, I received a very special gift. Isaac had just joined the Boy Scouts, and Adam was going to be the assistant leader for his troop. The night before the accident, we received his uniform in the mail and he tried it on. He looked so cute as he ran around the house ecstatic about his very official-looking uniform. Adam loved the Boy Scouts and told me that those were some of his fondest memories as a child. While watching Isaac run around in his uniform, Adam said, "You watch. Isaac will be our Eagle Scout." For Adam, that was one of the highest honors you could receive as a young man.

I received a call one day from a mom-friend, Lynee Fehler. She told me the Boy Scouts had a standard protocol in place that when one of the lives of their Scouts was taken early, then there was an opportunity for them to be recognized as an honorary Eagle Scout. She said that the decision was made in regard to Isaac, and he was being made an Honorary Eagle Scout. There would be a ceremony presenting the award to me in his stead. I was so touched that I could hardly speak. No one knew about the conversation Adam and I had the night before the wreck. But Adam was right—Isaac became our Eagle Scout.

The Lord was showing me with each child that they were not forgotten by him or the world. The healing continued.

Valentine's Day

Valentine's Day arrived, and I received one dozen red roses with a card that said, "I love you, Jesus." I was surprised by the unexpected arrival and had no clue who would have sent them. Adam may not have been a romantic all of the time, but he would always give me a dozen red roses on Valentine's Day. I received a call from my daughter Samantha asking if I had gotten the roses. The mother of one of her friends sent them to me. I called the mother to thank her and she told me she had known since Christmas that she was going to send them. It had been difficult for her to keep it a secret for so long. She said one day, while she was praying for my family, the Lord spoke to her and told her to send me a dozen red roses on Valentine's Day. Not only did she have no idea Adam always gave me a dozen red roses every year, it was also significant to understand that the red roses represent love. Once again, the Lord had a plan in place to let me know I was loved and not forgotten.

Blake

It was now April, six months since the accident, and the twenty-second was Blake's birthday. I can honestly say that of the four youngest kids, Blake had the sweetest, most sensitive nature. He was a little bashful and so adorable. Blake always thought about other people and was such a joy to be around. He was our baseball player. In his last season, Blake pitched a no hitter and hit a grand slam all in one game. It was a stellar night for him. The League City Little League showed so much compassion and honored our family in several different ways. They held a fundraiser for my family, put our family's name (all three boys played) in their hall of fame at the baseball field, and they made a logo for over one thousand uniforms that had a P with four little stars next to it, representing Adam and our four children, for the next season. I was also asked to throw out the first pitch on opening day for the following season—never mind that I'm not very good and almost took out the Board of Directors sitting in chairs on the field, nowhere near the catcher! But they were very gracious and gave me a second try, which turned out much better.

On Blake's birthday, a lady in my church walked up to me and handed me a letter. She had no idea it was his birthday. Her letter told me of how she'd been a teacher at Bay Area Christian's Vacation Bible School the summer of 2005, and Blake had been in her class. One day while they were at recess, Blake sat down for a moment to rest, and she sat down beside him to talk. She told me how sweet he was, and she knew he was a special little boy. When they got up from the quick break, Blake walked around the playground and picked up the trash without being asked to do so. She wanted me to know that Blake was not forgotten. By this time, I had begun to recognize the special gifts I was receiving for each holiday and my childens' birthdays. I was overwhelmed by the love the Lord was showing to me in each of these unique circumstances. It is his attention to the personal details of our lives that confirm his love towards us and bring healing and comfort.

Adam

It was now the beginning of June and eight months since the date of the accident. My and Adam's wedding anniversary was coming up on the sixth—D-Day. This proved to be a very difficult week, just like the other weeks, as I was dealing with each of my babies on an individual basis. I remembered when Adam and I were driving off after our wedding and heading to our honeymoon in San Antonio, he made this comment: "Baby, it is De-embarkment Day in the spirit—now we are partners in crime—stealing souls from the devil." We both knew that with prayer and living our lives for the Lord, we would lead many to Jesus.

I missed seeing his face, hearing his voice, snuggling on the couch, and the comfort of my husband in general. On the morning of my anniversary, at 6:00 a.m., the

Lord woke me up and said, "Zephaniah." ***What? Is this you Lord? Must be, because I am not a morning person, and I would have never told myself to get up at 6:00 a.m.*** I got up, got my Bible and began reading in the book of Zephaniah. I wasn't sure where to go to, so I just started at the beginning. When I got to chapter three, the Lord began speaking to me. Verse sixteen says, "He will quiet you with his love. He rejoices over you with singing." The Lord had kept me calm with his unconditional love, and when the Creator of the universe sings over you, no other voice can drown him out. Then in verse seventeen it says, "The sorrows for the appointed feasts I am removing from you because they are a burden and a reproach." Then all of the sudden, I felt this joy come over me, and I wanted to laugh out loud. The appointed feasts for the Jews were their holidays and the Lord had used the holidays to help me address the loss of each one of my family members. He had removed the heavy burden of the sorrows from me. I knew the Lord had completely healed my heart, and now it was my choice to believe in what he had done for me and walk in it.

My Thirty-Seventh Birthday

Eleven days after the Lord had completed the healing of my heart, I turned thirty-seven years old. Just eight months prior, at the age of thirty-six, I thought my life was over. I thought I was going to be trapped in a thirty-six year old healthy body for who knows how many years and suffer for the rest of my life without my husband and babies. Well, by the amazing grace, love, and power of my God, I was waking up at the age of thirty-seven with peace, joy, and hope.

As I lay there that morning, I knew I had decisions to make. I felt completely at rest, but I knew I could make a choice to be unhappy if I wanted to. Birthdays were always a big deal at our house. The kids would come bounding in with breakfast in bed (which would usually be cereal), wonderful homemade gifts, and plans for the day to bake a cake and probably go out to eat. Adam would always make sure on that day that everything was taken care of. No housework or chores of any kind. He would say, "this is your day, what would you like to do?" It would have been an easy thing to slip into self-pity and sadness, because instead of those things, I was lying there alone and had no special plans at all. I decided to embrace the promise from my God and be healed. And that is exactly what I was.

The Call

After the Lord set me free so quickly from the burden of the loss of Adam and the kids, I spent hours a day in worship and in his presence allowing him to heal my heart. When you get into the presence of God, He is going to start talking to you. I was a captive audience. The Lord began to take me back to the very beginning and give me understanding on what had taken place with each new revelation and told me that I was going to go and tell people what he had done. *What? Are you sure Lord? I think you might have the wrong girl!* Getting up in front of crowds and speaking was never my forte. I was the mom who wanted to stay behind the scenes and let everyone else be in the forefront. However, no one else could tell my story.

When God speaks to you, the Bible says he will confirm his Word in the mouth of two or three witnesses (Matthew 18:16). This is one way to test what you feel you have heard from God. I told the Lord, "I believe you, and I am willing to heed the call. After what you have done for me, there is nothing I will not do for you. But just show me, Lord. Give me evidence that what I am hearing is accurate." About a week before Christmas, I received a phone call from a friend, and she told me she'd been thinking of me every day. She began to inquire of the Lord what it was about. She told me that she believed it was because I was supposed to speak at her church (Witness number one).

In January, approximately three months after the accident, I received a phone call from a pastor who had attended our memorial service. He asked if I would be willing to share my testimony. He told me, "I'm not sure what happened. But I know that something happened." What he meant was that as he was attending our memorial service, he knew that the Lord was present and doing something in our lives. (Witness number two).

I set up a meeting with my pastor to discuss ministry. He spent some time talking to me about this type of ministry and told me he had expected ministry to be birthed from this situation in my life. He said that he affirmed me and considered my ministry as one under the covering of Abundant Life Christian Center. Now there was nothing holding me back. And thus began Dori Powledge Ministries.

The Not So Final Chapter

This will simply be the final chapter of my story… for now… because the Lord is definitely not through yet. I will give you a quick update, and then we can see where it goes from here.

It has been almost four years since the day I thought my life was completely over. I am now engaged to an incredibly wonderful, godly man who loves me with all of his heart. I met Toby at my church, about one year after the accident, when he came here to be the church drummer. We began dating about two-and-a-half years later. One evening, he took me to dinner at a beautiful restaurant in the Galleria area of Houston. I had a suspicion he was going to propose at dinner, but by the time we finished having dessert, I decided I must be wrong. As we were walking out of the restaurant, a beautiful horse and carriage came pulling up to give us a ride. Toby had thought of everything. He proposed on the carriage ride under a beautiful moonlit night. Sound like a familiar story? Sometimes our lives have a Cinderella beginning, but with Jesus, we can also have her happy ending.

The kids, P.J., twenty-two, Samantha, twenty-one, Amber, twenty, and Austin, eighteen, are all doing well and moving forward in their lives. They are continuing to learn and grow and accomplish, as well as gaining an understanding that it is up to each of us as individuals to make every day count. But most importantly, we are all continuing to live our lives according to the plans and purposes of God.

My hope and prayer at the conclusion of this book is that you come to the knowledge of the love of God, that Jesus become your Savior and Lord, and that you be free and healed, and live with hope for a beautiful future. With God, all things are possible!